Traditional, Country and Electric
Slide Guitar

by Arlen Roth

© Oak Publications, New York, 1975

Music Sales Limited, London

This book is lovingly dedicated to
my family and to my darling Janey

Special thanks to Jean Hammons, Jason Shulman
and Arthur Steinman for their fine editorial work
and constructive advice.

Cover design by Iris Weinstein

Book design by Jean Hammons

© Oak Publications
A Division of Embassy Music Corporation, 1975
33 West 60th Street, New York 10023

Music Sales Limited, 78 Newman Street, W1 London

Music Sales (Pty) Limited
27 Clarendon Street, Artarmon, Sydney NSW, Australia

International Standard Book Number 0-8256-0162-2
Library of Congress Card Catalog Number 74-21598

Contents

Photo Credits

Page	Guitarist	Photographer
14	Duane Allman	Courtesy of Capricorn Records
31	J. B. Hutto	Herb Wise
34	Bukka White	Herb Wise
36	Pete Drake	David Gahr
40	Fred McDowell	David Gahr
46	Mick Taylor	Beth Bagby
59	Peter Graves	David Gahr
61	Son House	David Gahr
67	Robert Pete Williams	Herb Wise
68	Tampa Red	Courtesy of Yazoo Records
72	Jimmie Tarlton	David Gahr
80	Richard Betts	Courtesy of Capricorn Records
82	Lloyd Green	Winnie Winston
84	Kayton Roberts	Winnie Winston
86	Bill Keith with Jim Kweskin's band	David Gahr
88	Homesick James	David Gahr
90	Rory Galleger	David Gahr
101	Speedy West	Herb Wise
106	Ry Cooder	Courtesy of Warner Brothers
126	Johnny Winter	Courtesy of Columbia Records
128	Arlen Roth	Janey Schram

All technical photos by Mark Stein
Cover photo by Ray Flerlage
Back cover photo by Janey Schram

Foreword

Over the past few years, the bottleneck guitar has become an increasingly popular means of expression among guitarists everywhere. In the rock and pop music fields some of the bottleneck's exponents have included Johnny Winter, Mick Taylor, Keith Richard, Duane Allman, George Harrison, Ry Cooder and many others. These people have all broadened the scope of the bottleneck guitar, but they owe a great deal to the true pioneers of this style of playing—Robert Johnson, Son House, Bukka White, Tampa Red, Fred McDowell, J. B. Hutto, and Elmore James, to name a few.

Son House, Robert Johnson, and Bukka White, were all of the traditional Southern folk-blues school of slide guitar. This era reached its height during the 1920's and the depression years. Later on, in the 40's and 50's, country people from the rural south began to move to the northern cities. Guitarists with their roots in the country blues soon discovered the electric guitar, and began to play with musical back-up musicians like bass and drums for a bigger, more "urbanized" sound.

In this book, we will cover all aspects of the bottleneck guitar, past and present, from the low-down bottleneck styles of the Mississippi Delta, to the present day lead guitar sounds.

To enable you to better understand these sounds, I have included an instruction record. All the material on the record is transcribed in the book to make it easier for you to follow along with what is being played.

Though the bulk of the material in this book will make use of open tunings, we'll get into some licks for playing slide in standard guitar tuning as well. There are plenty of blues licks, country licks and songs to work with, and feel free to improvise upon any of the musical ideas. After all, that's what this book, and music in general, is really all about.

By the time you've covered all the material, and feel really comfortable playing bottleneck, you should be well on your way towards developing your own approach towards the art of slide guitar. I certainly hope that you get a lot of mileage out of this book, but most of all, I hope you enjoy it, because it certainly was a pleasure for me to write.

—— Arlen Roth

Reading Tablature and Symbols

Tablature

For those of you who cannot read music, guitar tablature is provided below the standard musical notation. Tablature uses six lines representing the six strings of the guitar, with the bottom line as the low E, or sixth string. Here is how the tablature will appear:

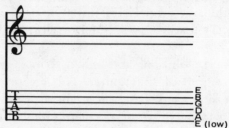

The numbers on the lines of the tablature correspond to the number of the fret at which your left hand depresses the string. For example, here is how a C chord would be illustrated:

Symbols:

A straight line pointing up or down *toward* a note means you slide *to* that note from an optional point below or above it. A straight line pointing down or up *away from* a note means you slide *from* the note without sounding another note after the slide:

An arched line tying two notes together with an *s* over it means you slide to the second note after picking the first note:

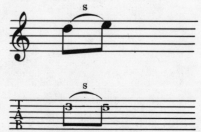

This same arched line with an *h* over it indicates a *hammer-on*:

If the arch appears with a *p* over it, it represents a left hand *pull off*:

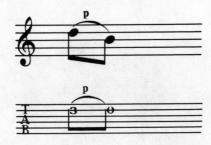

A *d* over a note in the tablature means you should dampen the note with your right hand as soon as you play the next note:

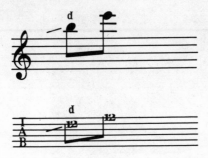

A note with a wavy line over it is played with vibrato:

Fundamentals of Slide Guitar Playing

Holding the instrument

When playing slide guitar is is important to be as comfortable as possible. Because the hand you are holding the slide on is not exerting as much pressure as if you were fretting in the normal fashion, the guitar sometimes has a tendency to get away from you. It is for this reason that your right arm and hand must hold the guitar more firmly to your body.

Of course if you're standing with the guitar and you're using a guitar strap, there is no problem as far as holding on to the guitar is concerned. You should, however, keep the neck a little higher than the rest of the guitar to avoid strain on your wrist while playing with a slide.

Setting up a guitar for slide

In setting up your guitar for playing with a slide, you will be trying to obtain the cleanest slide sound possible. To begin, the action should be raised high enough so that there is a minimum of fret buzz when using the slide, but not so high as to make fretting with your fingers unbearable. There is an attachment that dobro players use to raise the action called an *extension nut*. It fits over the nut of the guitar and raises the strings very high over the fingerboard. This creates a very clean slide sound, but its disadvantage lies in that it makes normal fretting with your fingers impossible.

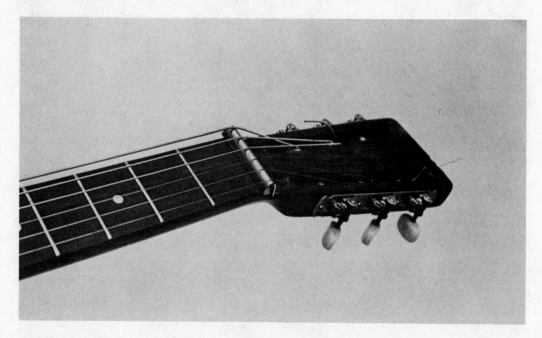

Strings

For playing bottleneck style your guitar strings should be of at least a medium gauge, especially for electric guitar because they will sustain notes longer, and resist the pressure of the slide more than light gauge strings.

Types of guitar for best results

Any steel-string guitar you now own, acoustic or electric, set up properly should be fine for learning slide playing. However, over the years, there are those guitars that have proven to be favorites among slide players.

The old country blues acoustic slide players almost always used National steel guitars. They are steel bodied resonator type guitars with a wide neck and a very crisp, metallic tone that lends itself readily to slide playing. Some of the bottleneck players past and present who used or now use National steels are: Tampa Red, Son House, Johnny Winter, Bukka White, Keith Richard, Black Ace, and Robert Johnson. (Photo of National Steel on next page.)

If you're going to play electric slide, you should try to have a guitar with good sustaining qualities. I prefer old Gibson Les Pauls and Fender Stratocasters.
(See photos on next page)

Some of the well-known modern slide players I have seen playing Les Pauls include Duane Allman and Mick Taylor. I've seen Stratocasters used for slide by George Harrison and Ry Cooder.

National steel

Fender Stratocaster and Gibson Les Paul

Choosing a slide

When looking for the proper slide you should make sure that it doesn't fit too tightly or loosely on your pinky. It should be long enough to cover all of the strings at each fret, but not so long and heavy as to make you feel clumsy. The kind of slide to use is a matter of personal taste. There are metal, glass, and ceramic slides that can be bought in music stores. I find that the metal slide gives you the loudest tone, while the glass slide produces the smoothest. The best thing to do is to try all of them and decide for yourself which one produces the best tone for your type of guitar.

Proper slide techniques—Holding the slide

Place the slide on your pinky and keep your thumb below the edge of the fingerboard on the back of the neck. Try to keep the slide perfectly perpendicular to the strings and parallel to the metal frets, as shown in the photo below:

Keep in mind that it isn't necessary to press down very hard on the strings to get a good sound with the slide. You should also lightly drag at least one of your other three fingers over the strings behind the slide to *dampen* any overtones that might occur while playing. See the photo below.

Open Tunings

Open tunings are used in slide guitar playing, and we will be working with the two most widely used tunings for bottleneck playing, often E tuning, and the A, or *Spanish* tuning.

The E tuning is as follows:

E B E G♯ B E

The underlined notes are the strings to be changed from normal guitar tuning:

E A D G B E

You can also tune the guitar the same way, only a whole step lower, thus making an open D tuning:

D A D F♯ A D

For the A, or *Spanish* tuning, you tune the guitar as follows:

E A E A C♯ E

The same tuning down of a whole step can be applied to get a G tuning:

D G D G B D

Now, assuming that you're comfortable enough with the slide and your guitar, let's start playing.

Duane Allman

14

Traditional Slide Guitar

Traditional slide guitar was usually played by the singer himself. This enabled him to do much in terms of phrasing between his voice and the guitar. This also illustrates that the original intention of bottleneck guitar was probably to simulate the lonesome, wailing sound of the human voice. Many times the singer would answer himself back and forth with the guitar, making the guitar "sing" by use of the slide. These singers would even use the bottleneck to imitate other sounds like the classic trainwhistle moan.

All of this points to the uncanny flexibility of bottleneck, and to its peculiar advantages, such as the ability to cut off notes, creating a special kind of staccato effect; achieving an unusual kind of vibrato over any number of strings desired, the ability to sound notes *between* half steps, and many others.

It is for these and other reasons that the bottleneck guitar remains as fresh a sound in today's music, as it was when it was first discovered.

Playing in Open E Tuning

Before we begin to play licks with the slide, we should concentrate on what your right hand, and the remaining three fingers on your left hand will be doing. Most traditional style bottleneck playing is usually a solo performance, and thereby necessitates the ability to use the slide without sacrificing the fullness and continuity of the piece you are playing. Obviously, when playing in an open tuning, the chord positions are now different from those in standard tuning. The first open tuning we will work with is open E; the diagrams that follow are the chord positions for this tuning:

Chord Positions in Open E Tuning

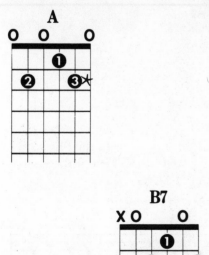

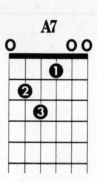

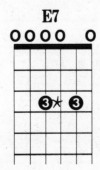

Of course, any major chord in E tuning may also be played by barring across the fret that corresponds to the name of the given barre chord:

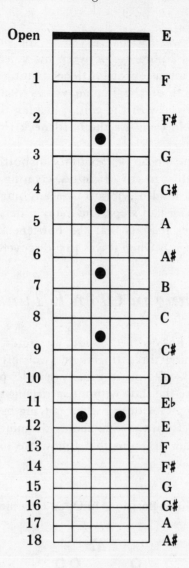

The twelve bar blues progression

The twelve bar blues is the most traditional and familiar form of the blues, and the majority of the material in this book will utilize this format. Here is the twelve bar blues in the key of E:

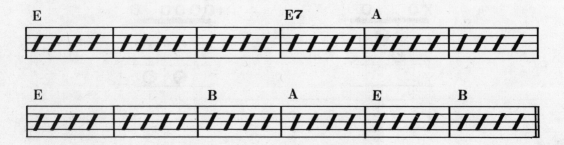

The three main chords used in this twelve bar progression were E, A and B. These are often referred to as the I, IV and V chords of the key of E. Simply defined, the I, or root chord is the chord with the same name as the key you are playing in. The IV, or sub-dominant chord's root is four notes away from and including the I chord in the scale of the particular key in which you are playing. The same definition applies to the V, or dominant chord.

The following diagram is a list of I, IV, and V chords.

List of I, IV and V Chords

I	IV	V
root	sub-dominant	dominant
A	D	E
A♯	D♯	F
B	E	F♯
C	F	G
C♯	F♯	G♯
D	G	A
D♯	G♯	A♯
E	A	B
F	A♯	C
F♯	B	C♯
G	C	D
G♯	C♯	D♯

The shuffle rhythm

If you have had a fair amount of experience playing blues guitar, the shuffle rhythm should come as no surprise to you. The only difference here is that because of the new tuning on your guitar, the positions of this rhythm-lick are now slightly altered. Here is the twelve bar blues progression in *E* using the shuffle rhythm:

The Shuffle Rhythm Lick in Open E Tuning

The next exercise is something I call the *Harmony Shuffle*. This is basically the same lick as the shuffle rhythm, except that the G string is now harmonizing with the notes played on the A, giving a fuller sound to the riff. The following are two examples of this rhythm to practice. One uses a straight flat-pick approach, and the other is in an alternating bass, fingerpicking style.

Harmony Shuffle-Flat-pick style

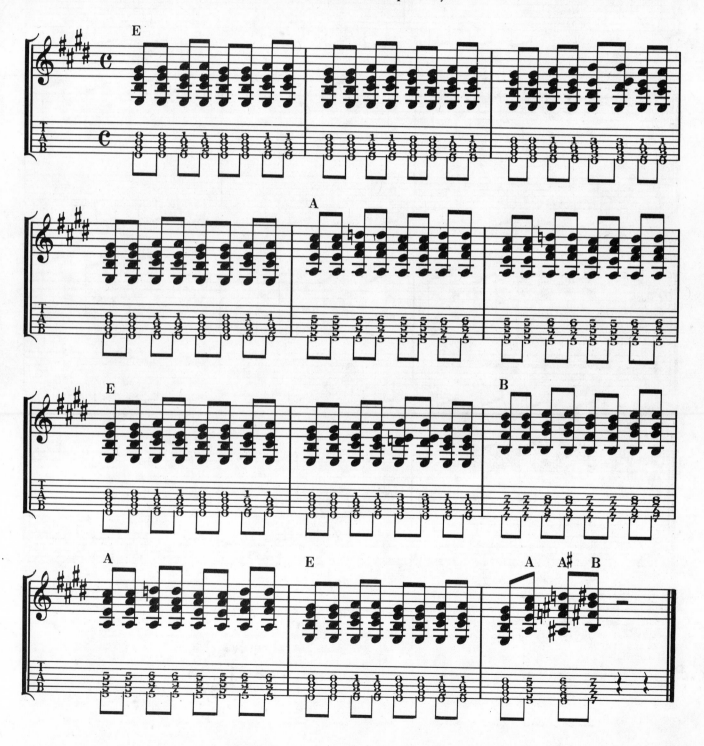

Using the slide

Now we'll finally start playing some basic licks to help you get into the feel of playing with a slide. In playing the traditional style of bottleneck, I highly recommend fingerpicking. If you are already a fairly experienced fingerpicker, and in a groove as far as where and when to use certain fingers, you should continue using the style you are most comfortable with. However, if you are new to fingerpicking, I recommend using your ring finger for the high E string, your middle for the B string, and your index finger for the G string. Your thumb should do all of the bass work, and licks incorporating the D, A, and low E strings should usually be played with the thumb and the index finger. Use all the proper slide techniques discussed in the previous chapter while playing the following exercises:

Basic Slide Exercises

In the first exercise, the line next to the B means you slide up to the note (twelfth fret) after picking the B string.

In the next exercise, we'll use the top three strings, tuned E, B and G♯. This time you begin the lick with a slide up to the twelfth fret on the G string.

Vibrato

In the following exercise we'll use the bottleneck with vibrato. This can be achieved by vibrating your hand back and forth very quickly, while at the same time trying to keep the slide from wandering too far from the note you are playing. For this lick we'll repeat the last exercise; when you reach the note with the vibrato sign (〰) over it, start the vibrato, while still allowing all three strings to vibrate, thereby creating a sustained chord.

You can also try sliding up to the three notes simultaneously, starting the vibrato when you reach the twelfth fret, creating a kind of *attacking* sound.

Here is a twelve bar blues exercise for bottleneck. Try to use the proper right hand fingering I have indicated below the tablature, and keep practicing until your fingers begin to feel comfortable playing in this position.

The constant bass

In traditional blues guitar, of which bottleneck is an offshoot, bass notes and rhythms become an essential tool by which continuity in a solo piece of music may be achieved. In this next twelve bar exercise, you'll be playing the same licks as in the previous exercise, except that you will be playing a constant bass rhythm throughout the piece. The bass rhythm will be the same as the shuffle we previously worked on in this chapter. Keep in mind that when you play the A chord (fifth fret), your slide should cover all the strings so that you can sound the A bass cleanly. If your slide isn't long enough, I would suggest finding a longer slide which I consider superior for all slide work anyway.

Constant Bass Exercise

Blues scales

The blues box pattern

Through my own playing I have found that these two basic blues scales are the most economic positions for playing blues licks in E tuning. The first scale begins at the twelfth fret (for the key of E), and I call it the blues *box pattern*. Here it is in notation and a diagram, and when practicing it use the slides between notes as I have indicated.

Box Pattern Scale

Blues Box Pattern—E Tuning

Strings tuned to:

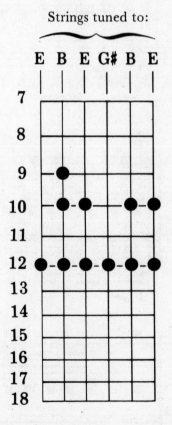

24

The other blues scale is the *open position* scale which utilizes some open strings. The notes in parentheses are alternate positions for the open string notes.

Open Position Scale

Open Position Scale

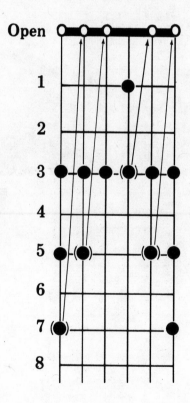

NOTE: Dots in parenthesis indicate substitute notes for open string notes

Licks in E tuning

There are many blues licks within the *box pattern* and the *open position* scales, and the following licks are based on these two positions. When practicing these licks try to maintain the proper right hand technique previously discussed. Also a word about damping strings with your picking hand; if the lick moves toward the high E string and you desire to dampen certain strings, you should use your thumb for this. If the lick moves in the opposite direction, you should dampen the strings with the same fingers that plucked them.

Licks and Exercises in Open E Tuning

In this first *box pattern* lick, try to dampen the strings with the same fingers that plucked them. The notes with a *d* over them in the tablature are the notes you should dampen:

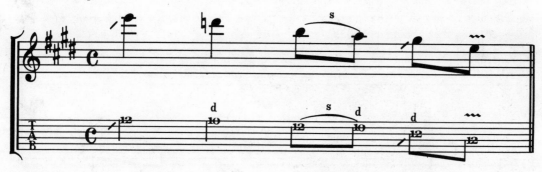

Here is the same lick, except that in this one you end up on the E that is one octave bigger than the one before:

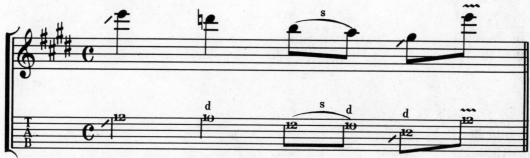

This lick is the same blues run as the last two, only played an octave lower. This run, together with the two previous ones, completes the *box pattern* scale:

You can try the same lick as part of the *open position* scale:

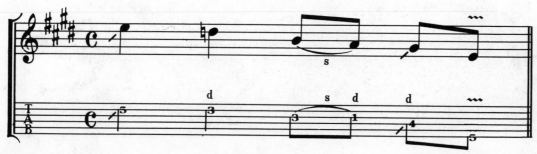

This next run ventures away from the *box pattern* slightly, and keep in mind that the right hand damping is not to create a stacatto effect, but rather to stop a string from vibrating at precisely the same time you pluck another string. This style of damping will enable you to achieve a very smooth single-string slide technique:

This lick has a nice mellow country blues sound, and is frequently heard in old-time slide playing. You can try it without damping, which also sounds good:

This lick should have more of an *attacking* sound to it, achieved by sliding up very quickly at the beginning. The first damp should be on the high E string only, enabling you to slide down on the B string to the tenth fret:

The damping in the next lick is a bit tricky. You must dampen the G string as you dampen the E, leaving the B string free for the slide down to the tenth fret. This can be achieved by damping the G string with your thumb and the E string with your ring finger.

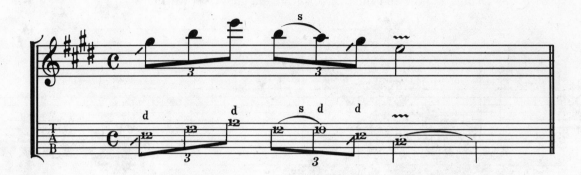

In this *open position* lick we'll use our first *pull off*. This means that as you start the lick on the A string, fifth fret, you slide down to the third fret and without plucking the string again, pull the slide off the string. Doing this will sound the open A string. For the best sound, I would recommend pulling the slide off while still in the downward motion of the lick. This will vibrate the string more than lifting the slide straight up off the string.

The following exercises will explore some of the many possibilities for solo bottleneck playing in open E tuning. I have written these pieces with the development of your right hand technique as well as your bottleneck skill in mind. They all utilize the twelve bar, I, IV, V blues format, and include the *box pattern* and *open position* blues licks that you have already pacticed, plus some new ones as well. In the pieces that include a constant bass, really concentrate on keeping the rhythm flowing smoothly. The ideal situation will be when your right hand is working so well that you sound almost like a lead slide player with another guitarist backing you up with strong bass notes.

Exercise 1

This first piece uses a constant bass throughout, except at the end of the sixth measure, where you play a *fill* that leads you into the E chord of the next measure. This is a dramatic effect used by many country blues slide players, and we will work with this technique now and then throughout the course of this book.

J. B. Hutto

Exercise 2—The turnaround lick

In this next constant bass exercise we will be using a *turnaround* lick for the first time. This lick occurs during the last two bars in a twelve bar blues and serves to *turn* the song around and start the progression all over again. Two familiar licks we will be using as turnarounds are as follows:

Turnaround Licks

The second *turnaround* lick may also be played an octave higher:

Of course, these *turnarounds* are really just another type of blues lick, and they don't always have to be used exclusively during the last two measures of a blues progression. We will be playing other fills and licks as turnarounds throughout the book as well, and in the next exercise a turnaround lick is used as an introduction.

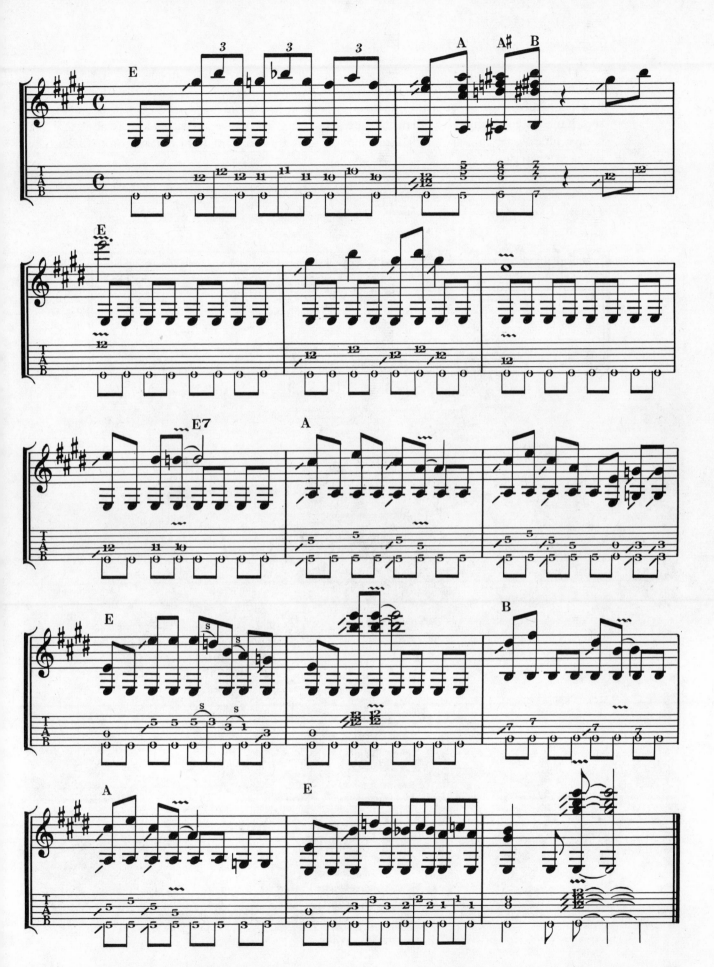

Exercse 3—Double string harmonies and octave licks

This next exercise comprises several licks that use two strings played simultaneously, or what I refer to as *double string harmony* licks. Additionally, the tenth measure consists of a double string octave run. This means that you will be simultaneously playing two identical notes that are an octave apart. Below is an octave blues scale to help familiarize yourself with this concept before going on to the next exercise:

Octave Exercise

Bukka White

34

Exercise 4

Of all the exercises you've played so far, the following should present the most difficulty. Not that I think you can't master it, but because it incorporates practically everything we've covered so far. This entire piece should be approached with an *attacking* style, and frequently makes use of the dramatic *fill* effect that we touched upon in Exercise 1. Therefore, I would venture to call it the most "theatrical" piece of music we've covered so far. Go ahead and enjoy it!

Pete Drake

Exercise 5

The styles of the country blues slide men, especially that of Robert Johnson, influenced me in writing this exercise. There are many more "angry" sounding bass string licks in this one, and there is only one measure that includes a constant bass accompaniment. Four *pull-offs* are also included in this piece, and each one follows a slide on the same string you pull the slide off of. Keep in mind that you should pull the slide off in the same downward direction as the note of the lick:

Exercise 6—New turnaround lick using tilting of the slide

Tilting the slide to play two or more notes on different frets is a common technique employed by dobroists and Hawaiian Steel players. Personally, I have never seen a bottleneck player using this technique before, because it is too difficult to bend your wrist in all the angles these licks dictate. There is, however, one position and a turnaround lick I have arrived at that requires only a little pain! If you're playing on a guitar without a cutaway, or with a neck that joins the body at the twelfth fret, tilting the slide will be a little tougher when playing this lick at the sixteenth fret as I have notated. Here is the way to play the beginning of this lick on such a guitar. Note the position of the hand for the most freedom of movement, and the positioning of the slide directly over the fifteenth and sixteenth frets:

Now here's the *turnaround*:

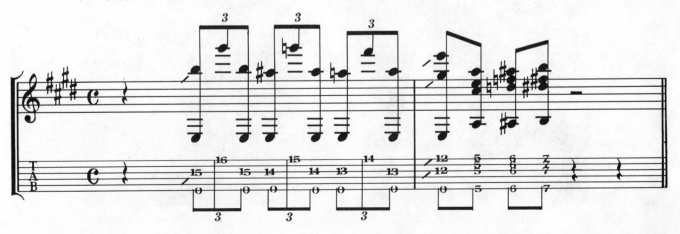

In the second measure after the intro, another dobro technique is borrowed entailing a slide on the D string while playing the open B string as a harmony. The only tricky part in playing this lick is lifting the slide and making sure that it clears all the other strings except the D string, enabling the open B to be sounded cleanly. We'll make a more thorough investigation of this technique later on, in the section on country bottleneck.

Fred McDowell

Turnaround Lick With Slide Tilt

Playing in Open G Tuning

Open G tuning has always been widely used in the traditional bottleneck medium. One of this tuning's most unique and attracting qualities is its banjo-like sound due to its relatively high open pitch. This effect becomes even more apparent if you tune it up a whole step higher to A tuning, another popular version of G tuning, (if your guitar's neck can take it!). We'll cover, quite thoroughly, the many possibilities for traditional bottleneck in open G and I'll cite several aspects relevant to both E and G tunings as we go along.

Here are some chord positions in open G or A tuning. Note that the positions for these chords are the same as in open E, but that each note is moved to the next higher string than before:

Chord Positions in Open G(or A) Tuning

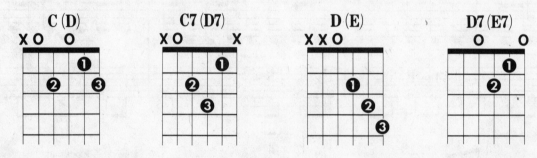

Blues scales

There is also a *box pattern* and an open position scale for blues in G tuning, and they relate to the similar scales for open E already discussed:

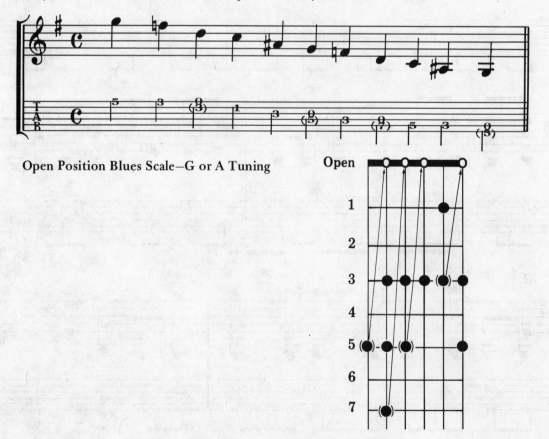

Open Position Blues Scale—G or A Tuning

Blues Box Pattern—G or A Tuning

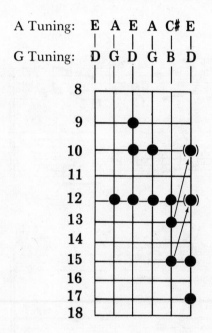

A Tuning: E A E A C# E

G Tuning: D G D G B D

Licks and Exercises in Open G Tuning

Blues licks

The following is a list of some of the blues licks in open G that you should become familiar with before going on to the rest of the chapter. Remember that all of these positions apply to open A tuning as well:

Octave blues scale

Playing octave licks in G tuning is a little easier than in E tuning. This is due to the fact that open G has two octaves that are only divided by one string, where open E has only one octave one string apart, and two that are divided by two strings. Here is the octave blues scale for open G or A tuning:

Turnaround licks

The first three turnaround licks shown below are all positioned the same as the *turnarounds* we discussed for open E, but the fourth one is unique to this tuning:

Exercises

The next five exercises are written with the assumption that both your slide work and right hand technique are already fairly sophisticated. If you feel that this is not the case, you should go back and practice the pieces for E tuning, until you are satisfied with the results. Remember that learning slide guitar should be a relatively slow and deliberate process, so try not to feel too frustrated if it takes several attempts at a piece before you can settle down into a groove.

Exercise 1

This is a fairly easy exercise, designed to help you to get into playing a constant bass in open G while at the same time playing some relatively familiar blues licks.

Mick Taylor

47

This piece uses a constant bass only sparsely, while concentrating mainly upon the single string riff style heard so often in the playing of the great country blues slide artists.

Exercise 3

The next exercise has more of a country sound to it, mainly due to the licks using the major third (B), for the key of G, rather than the minor third (A#), as in most blues scales.

49

Exercise 4—The stop-time lick

The first three measures in this exercise are led into by what I call a *stop-time* lick. This lick consists first of a slide up to the tonic note (G), and then quickly playing the open G an octave lower, and damping it for the *stop-time* effect. This lick is heard in the playing of Son House and Robert Johnson, among others.

Exercise 5

This piece has an interesting octave lick introduction, and concentrates on playing triplets on the treble strings, while maintaining the constant bass.

Traditional Bottleneck Tunes In Open E Tuning

Assuming that you've now covered all of the material in the previous chapters and feel fairly comfortable playing slide guitar, we should begin to put this knowledge to use in some songs. Most of the tunes in this chapter will have accompaniment and breaks based on the playing of two great traditional slide players, Robert Johnson and Tampa Red. However, in order to further expound upon the exercises and licks I have thus far shown to you, I have also arranged a traditional non-bottleneck blues song, *Good Morning Blues*, according to some of my own ideas on slide playing.

Keep practicing these tunes over and over again, and try to put a little more of yourself into it each time you play. After awhile, you should be able to come up with some new licks and ideas of your own, and that's when you'll really start to accomplish something.

Good Morning Blues

For this song we'll use a shuffle rhythm accompaniment during the singing, and a constant bass during the fills, turnarounds, and while playing the solo. Try to work hard on maintaining the constant bass while playing these licks.

Open E Tuning

Traditional. Arranged and adapted by Arlen Roth

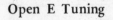

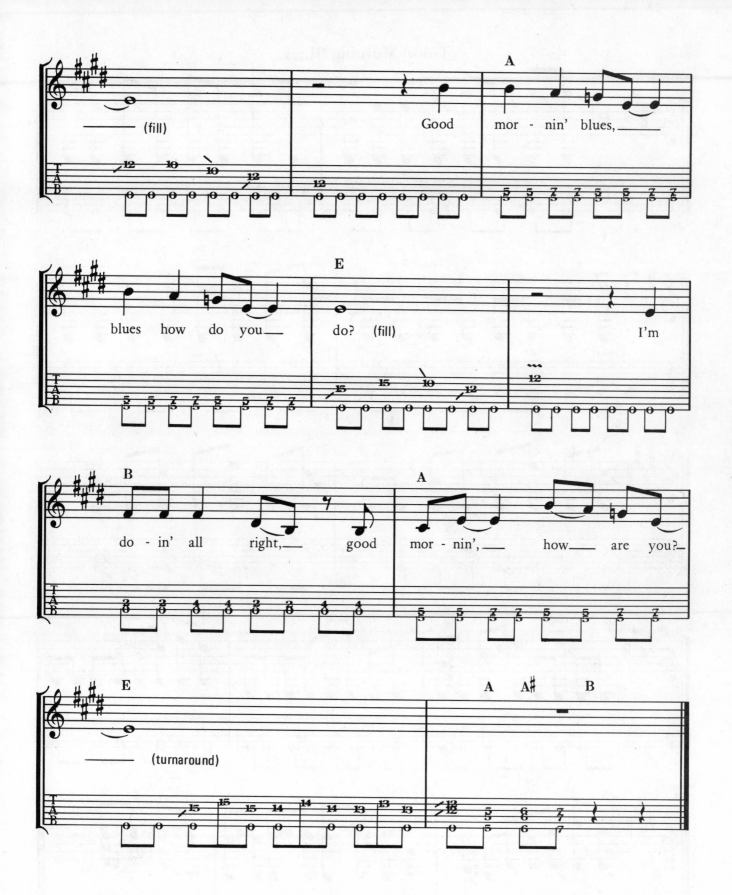

* Use <u>shuffle rhythm</u> on all eighth notes in this book.

Good Morning Blues

Ramblin' On My Mind

This next song is by Robert Johnson, probably the most important blues man who ever lived. He recorded it in 1936, and I transcribed (as accurately as I could), his guitar part from the Columbia album, *Robert Johnson, King of the Delta Blues Singers, Volume I.* Johnson alternates between normal fretting and bottlenecking, only going to the slide for some haunting moments during his singing, and as fills. Johnson doesn't take an instrumental solo on the record, so I've written out a break that is similar to his style for you.

Open E Tuning

Robert Johnson

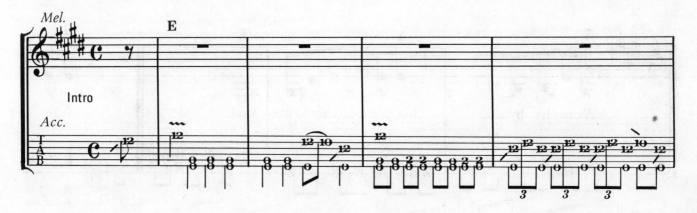

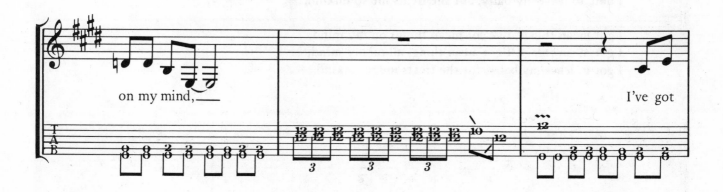

Fine   *D. S. al Fine*

I got mean things, I got mean things all on my mind,
Little girl, little girl, I got mean things all on my mind,
Hate to leave you here, babe, but you treats me so unkind.

Runnin' down to the station, catch the first mail train I see,
(*Spoken*: I think I hear her comin' now.)
Runnin' down to the station, catch that old first mail train
You see, I've got the blues 'bout Miss so-an'-so, and the child has got the blues 'bout me.

An' I'm leavin' this mornin' with my arms fold up an' cryin', (2x)
I hate to leave my baby, but she treats me so unkind.

I got mean things, I've got mean things on my mind,
I got mean things, I got mean things all on my mind,
I got to leave my baby, for she treats me so unkind.

Ramblin' On My Mind

If I Had Possession Over Judgement Day

This Robert Johnson classic in open G tuning was also transcribed from the *King of the Delta Blues Singers, Volume 1*. Johnson does a bit more slide work in this tune, but once again you'll have to settle for a solo by me!

Open G Tuning

As played by Robert Johnson

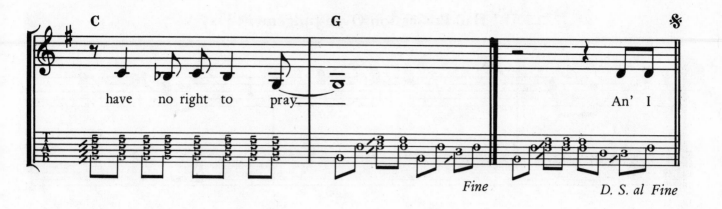

have   no right to   pray _____   An' I

Fine   *D. S. al Fine*

An' I went to the mountain, looked as far as my eyes could see, (2x)
Some other man got my woman, an' these lonesome blues got me.

An' I rolled an' I tumbled an' I cried the whole night long, (2x)
Boy, I woke up this mornin', my biscuit roller gone.

Had to fold my arms, an' I slowly walked away,
(*Spoken*: I didn't like the way she'd done.)
Had to fold my arms, an' I slowly walked away,
I felt in my mind your trouble gonna come someday.

Now, run here, baby, set down on my knee, (2x)
I wanna tell you all about the way they've treated me.

Peter Graves

If I Had Possession Over Judgement Day

Break

Son House

Preachin' Blues

Here is Robert Johnson's version of Son House's 1930 recording of *Preachin' The Blues*. It's played with a fast attack alternating between the high E and B strings and the bass strings. When played as fast as Johnson did it, this piece is quite difficult, so don't hesitate to get funky with it.

Open E Tuning

Robert Johnson

I was up this morn-ing, I got

blues walk-ing like a man.

I was up this morn-ing my

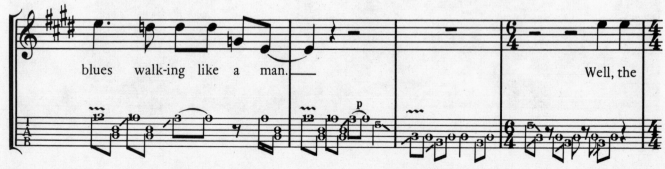

blues walk-ing like a man. Well, the

blues_____   give me   your   right   hand.

1.

2.

And the

And the blues fell, mama child, and they tore me all upside down,
Blues fell, mama child, and they tore me all upside down,
Travel on, poor Bob, just can't turn you 'round.

The blues is a low-down stinkin' gyp,
Ummh—is a low-down stinkin' gyp,
You ain't never had 'em, I hope you never will.

Well, the blues is a achin' old heart disease,
(*Spoken*: "Do it now, you gonna do it.")
The blues is a low-down, achin' heart disease,
Like consumption, killin' me by degrees.

Now if it starts a-rainin', oh drive, oh, oh drive my blues,
Now if it starts a-rainin' I'm gonna drive my blues away,
Goin' to Steeray, stay out there all day.

Come On In My Kitchen

This song illustrates Johnson's brilliant use of the bottleneck in unison with his vocal, a technique employed by many of the early country blues, and later Chicago blues, slide artists. Again, Johnson does not take a solo on his recording; therefore, I've written out a break similar in style to his accompaniment.

Open G Tuning

Robert Johnson

Uumh _____ uumh _____ uumh _____

_____ uumh _____ You bet-ter come on in my

kitch-en, Well, it's go - in' to be rain- in' out doors; _____

The wom-an I love, _____

Fine

64

took from my best friend,   some jok - er got

luck - y   stole her   back a - gain.   (goes back to) "You bet - ter come"

D. S. al Fine

Boy she's gone, I know she won't come back,
I taken the last nickel out of her ration sack.
You better come on in my kitchen, it's going to be rainin' outdoors.
(*Spoken twice:* "Oh can't you hear that wind howlin'.")
You better come on in my kitchen, it's goin to be rainin' outdoors.

And the time's comin', it's goin' be so,
You can't make the winter, babe, just try long so.
You better come on in my kitchen, it's going to be rainin' outdoors.

Come On In My Kitchen

Robert Pete Williams

Denver Blues

   Denver Blues was recorded by Tampa Red, the most prolific of all country blues bottleneck artists. Tampa Red is undoubtedly my all-time favorite, and I would strongly recommend picking up on his recordings if you want to hear some of the sweetest slide around. This song was recorded in 1934, and is on the Yazoo album, *Tampa Red, Bottleneck Guitar*. One of the few instrumental pieces recorded by Tampa Red, *Denver Blues* illustrates his beautiful phrasing and single string technique.

Tampa Red

Bumblebee Blues

Another great Tampa Red slide piece, *Bumblebee Blues*, recorded in 1931, contains some of the most interesting bottleneck work ever recorded. It was transcribed from the Yazoo album, *Guitar Wizard*. Enjoy it!

Open E Tuning

As played by Tampa Red

Instrumental

71

Country Slide Guitar

It is probably no secret to you by now that country music has had and is still having a tremendous influence on all of contemporary music. There are basically three *slide* instruments that are an integral part of the country sound; the *dobro,* *Hawaiian steel*, and the *pedal steel* guitar. All of these instruments are currently enjoying an increase in popularity, and bottleneck guitarists who have been into the blues style are now picking up on the country sounds as well. My experience with playing these instruments over the past few years has served to broaden my understanding of bottleneck guitar, and in this section I would like to share with you what I have found.

A few of the main differences between this style of bottlenecking and the blues style talked about in previous sections are: the use of sustaining open-string notes with overlapping, harmonizing notes; evidence of more double string harmony licks; and the use of an alternating bass rather than a constant one, in solo pieces. There are, of course, also many similarities between these two styles which will become more apparent to you as you play through this section. Therefore, your already substantial knowledge of bottleneck blues guitar should serve to help you approach these country pieces with the confidence of an experienced slide player who wishes to expand upon his or her own style of playing.

Jimmie Tarlton

Playing In Open E Tuning

Here is a scale in open E, from which most of the country licks in this chapter are formed:

Country Pattern

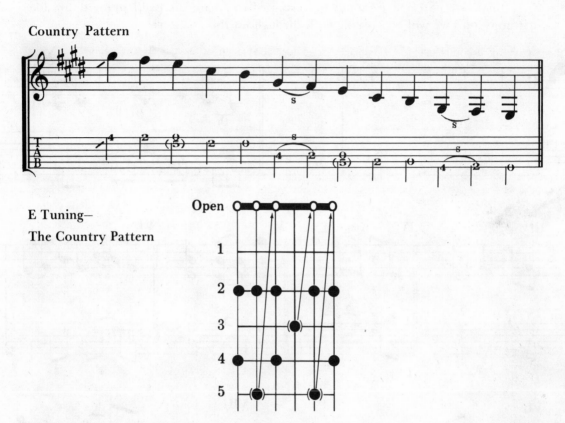

E Tuning—

The Country Pattern

You can also try this scale an octave higher, as follows:

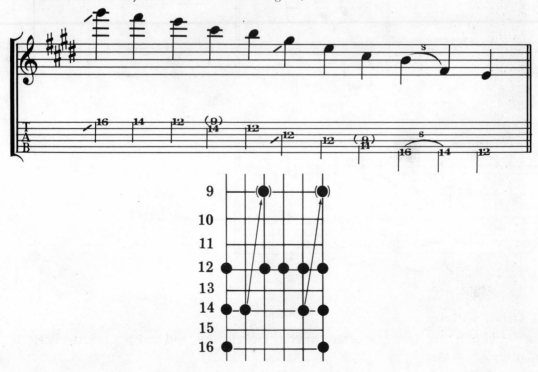

Licks and Exercises in Open E Tuning

Country Licks

The following is a group of country runs to practice. The notes with an asterisk over them are notes that should be sustained to create the overlapping dobro-like harmony runs we will be working with throughout this chapter:

Octave Exercise

We will also use some octave licks in this chapter, and here is a country scale in octaves:

Exercise 1—The alternating bass

In this chapter, most of the bass note rhythms we will be using are of the alternating kind. This involves an alternation between the D and low E strings (both tuned to E), at one bass note per beat. Hence, a four beat measure would consist of two alternations. Now, here is an exercise to help you become better acquainted with this technique:

Exercise 2—Syncopation

This exercise gets a little more complicated by syncopating treble notes between the alternating bass notes. Keep working on getting the bass rhythm to flow smoothly, and in no time, you should be able to sneak those lead notes in without a problem:

Exercise 3—Dobro-style licks

This exercise is really just a series of licks that utilize open strings for harmonies, a technique used by dobro players. Make sure to raise the slide high enough to clear the open strings, while keeping the slide only on the string that requires it.

Here are two photos of the proper slide positions for playing the high E string alone, and for playing a lower string alone:

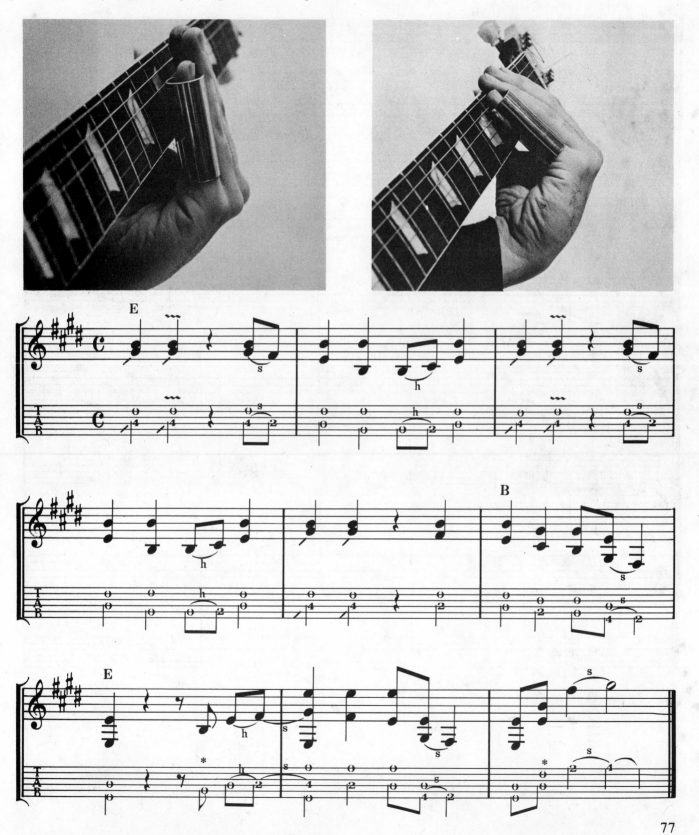

Exercise 4

This piece should eventually be played at a pretty fast clip, but practice it slowly at first. It is also the first exercise to make use of an open-string harmony lick for the A chord.

Exercise 5

Having another guitarist to accompany you (or a tape recording of a rhythm guitar part if you're playing by yourself), would be a helpful aid in playing this final country exercise in open E. You might also try playing it with an alternating bass, stopping the bass part to play the octave runs.

Now, if you feel fairly adept at playing country slide in open E tuning, we'll go on to some country songs.

Country Bottleneck Tunes in Open E Tuning

JOHN HENRY

There have been many different interpretations of this classic folk song, including several instrumental versions. Here is a bottleneck variation I've arranged, utilizing an alternating bass picking style in open E tuning.

Richard Betts

John Henry

Open E Tuning

Traditional.
Arranged and adapted by Arlen Roth

Bury Me Beneath The Willow

For this song I have written an accompaniment for the verses, and an instrumental break. The solo retains the same alternating bass as in the accompaniment, with an added melody line on top.

Open E Tuning

Traditional. Arranged and adapted by Arlen Roth

Bur - y me be - neath the

Lloyd Green

My heart is sad and I am lonely
Thinking of the one I love,
Will I meet her?—oh no never
Till we meet in heaven above.

She told me that she dearly loved me
How could I believe her untrue?
Until the day some neighbors told me
She has proven untrue to you.

Tomorrow was to be our wedding
I pray, Oh Lord, where can she be?
She's gone, she's gone to love another
She no longer cares for me.

Kayton Roberts

Bury Me Beneath The Willow

Farther Along

This beautiful country gospel song in waltz time works well with the few haunting slide runs I've sparingly placed during the verses, but you should feel free to experiment with other fills as you go along. The instrumental solo closely follows the melody of the song, and also leaves much room for improvisation.

Open E Tuning

Traditional. Arranged and adapted by Arlen Roth

Far – ther a – long   we'll   know all a – bout

it,   Far – ther a – long   we'll

Bill Keith with Jim Kweskin's band

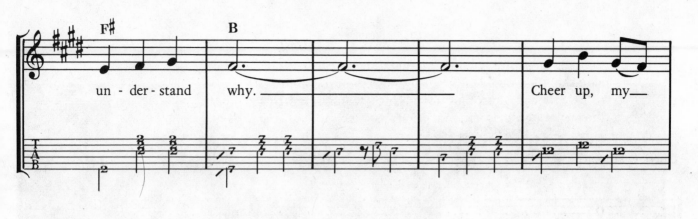

un - der - stand   why. _____   Cheer up, my ___

bro - thers,   live   in   the   sun - shine,

We'll   un - der - stand   it   all   by   and   by.

Tempted and tried we're oft made to wonder,
Why it should be thus all the day long,
While there are others living about us,
Never molested though in the wrong.

Often I wonder why I must journey,
Over a road so rugged and steep,
While there are others living in comfort,
While with the lost I labor and weep.

When death has come and taken our loved ones,
Leaving our homes so lone and so drear,
Then do we wonder why others prosper,
Living as sinners year after year.

Homesick James

Farther Along

Break

Will The Circle Be Unbroken?

This old-time country gospel song has been written out with a slide accompaniment that closely follows the melody line. Practice it slowly at first, and speed it up when you feel comfortable playing the alternating basses with the melody. The instrumental break I have written is similar to the accompaniment and utilizes several open-string *dobro* harmonies with the lead line.

Open E

Traditional. Arranged and adapted by Arlen Roth

Rory Galleger

90

Will the circle be unbroken
By and by Lord, by and by.
There's a better home awaiting,
In the sky Lord, in the sky.

Will The Circle Be Unbroken?

Playing in Open A(G) Tuning

For this chapter, I have chosen to work with open A, rather than the previously utilized open G tuning, because its high-pitched, banjo-like sound is more suited to the country sound. If you are playing an electric guitar, make sure that your strings are of a light enough gauge to take the high tension of this tuning. However, I would not recommend using this tuning if you are playing an acoustic guitar due to the high strain on the neck. Therefore, when playing acoustically you should tune to open G, and transpose accordingly.

Country scales in Open A (G) tuning

This first scale is the basic country pattern we will be working with. Make sure to play the slides between notes as I have indicated.

Dobro scale

This is the same scale except that each note is played with an open string harmony. When playing the slides between notes, strike the open string harmony with the first note, allowing it to ring as you slide to the second, creating a sustaining harmony over two notes.

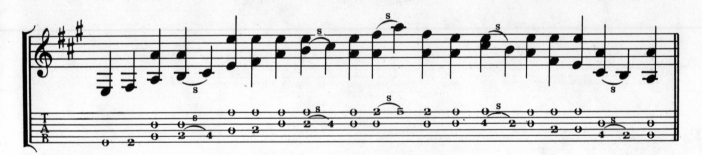

Licks and Exercises in Open A(G) Tuning

Country licks

The following group of country licks are just a few of the many possible runs that can be played in this tuning. As you practice them, try to play at a pretty fast clip, for this is the tempo at which most country licks are at their best.

Country octave lick

Here is a country octave run for A or G tuning. Notice again that this tuning lends itself more readily towards octave run playing than open E.

Exercise 1

This first exercise requires a good deal of right hand damping, and some careful slide angling to clear open strings for sustained harmonies.

Exercise 2

This piece is comprised mostly of octave licks. It should have a nice, funky feel to it when played in its proper spirit. The playing of Ry Cooder, a truly great slide man, influenced the writing of this exercise.

Exercise 3

If you should ever hear Cajun music from Louisiana you might notice that the fiddle player is playing a part quite similar to the sound of this next exercise. I thought it might be an interesting technique to try for slide guitar, and it ended up working out nicely.

Exercise 4

This piece is similar in feel to the first exercise in this section, but more complex. Make sure to let those open bass strings ring, while you hammer-on and slide up on the G string, creating a very full sounding dobro-style lick.

Country Bottleneck Tunes in Open A(G) Tuning

Brown's Ferry Blues

This old-time song is a great one for fast picking, and I have written out the instrumental break in a dobro-lick style employing open string harmonies. You should also note that while the fifth and thirteenth measures temporarily change to $\frac{6}{4}$ time during the verses, the instrumental solo remains $\frac{4}{4}$ throughout.

Brown's Ferry Blues

Open A Tuning

Traditional. Arranged and adapted by Arlen Roth

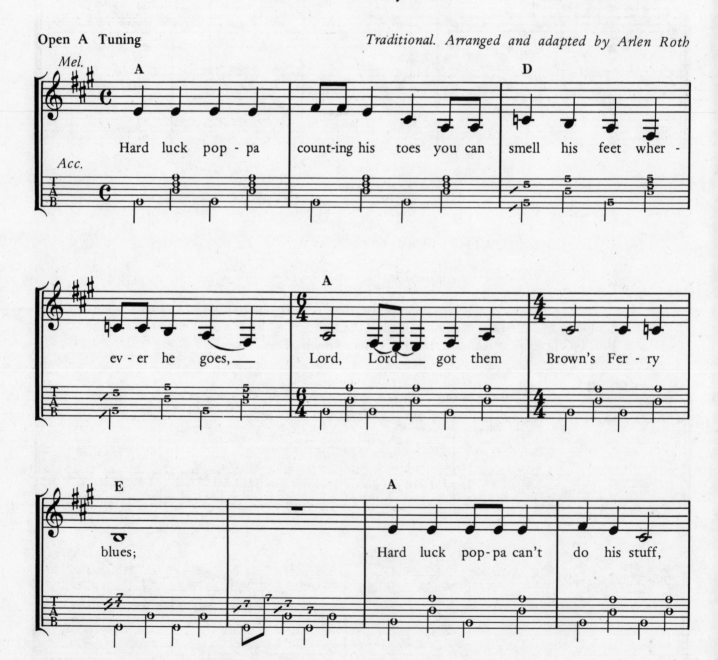

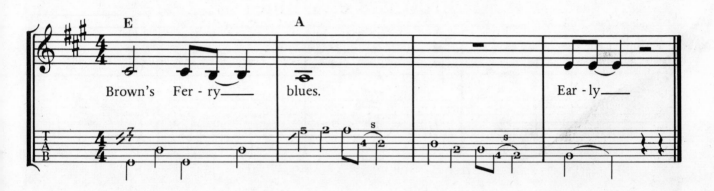

Early to bed and early to rise
And your girl goes out with other guys,
Lord, Lord got them Brown's Ferry Blues.

If you don't believe me try it yourself
Well I tried, and I got left,
Lord, Lord got them Brown's Ferry blues.

Hard luck Poppa standing in the rain
If the world was corn, he couldn't buy grain,
Lord, Lord got them Brown's Ferry blues

Hard luck Poppa standing in the snow
His knees knock together but he's raring to go,
Lord, Lord got them Brown's Ferry blues.

Brown's Ferry Blues

Break

Speedy West

Danville Gal

This $\frac{3}{4}$ time country song should be played at an easy-going pace. Try playing the solo with a sparse, melancholy approach. I've arranged this tune in open G because I find that it lends itself more readily to the sound of an acoustic guitar.

Open G Tuning

Traditonal. Arranged and adapted by Arlen Roth

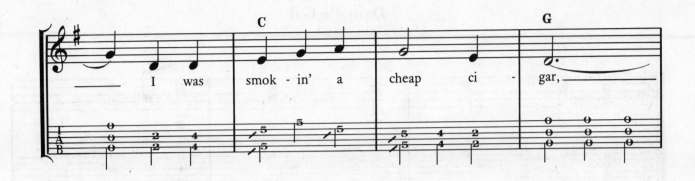

I was smok-in' a cheap ci - gar,

Lis - t'nin' for the next freight

train, to car - ry an emp - ty car.

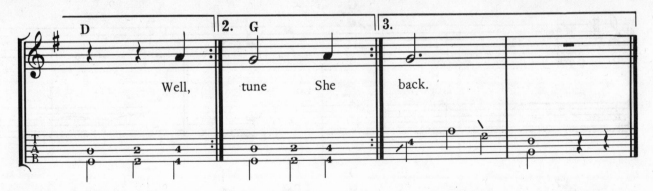

Well, tune She back.

I got off at Danville,
Got stuck on a Danville girl,
You can bet your life she was out-of-sight,
She wore those Danville curls.
She took me in her kitchen
And treated me nice and kind,
But she got me in the notion
Of bumming all the time.

She wore her hat on back of her head,
Like the high-toned people do,
So the very next train come down the track,
I bade that girl adieu.
I pulled my cap down over my eyes,
And walked down to the track,
Then I caught a railroad car,
Never did look back.

Danville Gal

How Can You Keep On Movin'

Ry Cooder, one of the greatest contemporary slide players, recorded an excellent version of this song on his Reprise album, *Into the Purple Valley*. Cooder plays it with a real funky country flavor, and in the accompaniment and break I have tried to capture his unique sound.

Open A Tuning   *Traditional. Arranged and adapted by Arlen Roth*

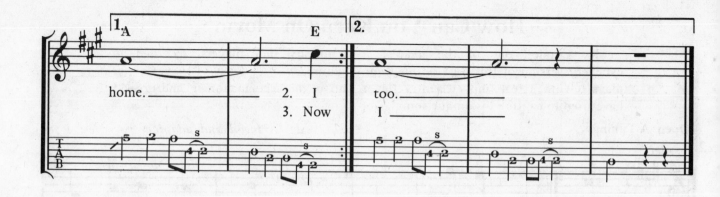

I can't go back to the homestead, the shack no longer stands
They said I wasn't need, had no claim to the land
They said "Come on, get movin', it's the only thing for you"
But how can you get movin' unless you migrate too.

Now, if you pitch your little tent along the broad highway
The Board of Sanitation says "Sorry, you can't stay."
"Come on, come on, get movin'," it's their ever-lasting cry
Can't stay, can't go back and can't migrate so where in hell am I?

Ry Cooder

How Can You Keep On Movin'

Break

Lead Electric Slide Guitar

Playing bottleneck with an electric guitar can be a very different experience from playing acoustically. An amplified guitar has greater sustaining capabilities and of course sounds louder than an acoustic guitar, therefore creating new and subtler tone possibilities. If you listen to any of the modern lead guitarists who use slides such as Duane Allman, George Harrison, Ry Cooder, Johnny Winter, etc., you should notice the frequent utilization of longer, more drawn out slides between notes due to the sustaining power of an electric guitar.

Obviously, slide playing has become an important facet of lead guitar, and has changed quite a bit over the years, but the original country blues bottleneck players are still at the root of the sounds we hear today. Elmore James, or "Elmo" James, the great post-war Chicago blues man, was probably the first slide player to use an electric guitar with any real success. James played in an emotional, hard-driving style that was influenced by the playing of Robert Johnson, the Delta blues man. Elmore James' most important recording was that of an old Robert Johnson song called *I Believe I'll Dust My Broom*. His version of this song was so popular that James called his back-up band the "Broomdusters". James' playing in this song has become the most imitated and emulated of all electric slide licks.

Dust My Broom

Due to its powerful influence on electric bottleneck guitar, *Dust My Broom* will be the first exercise in this section. The solo is based on the style of Elmore James, and should also be used as an intro before the first verse. Although it can be played in a fingerpick style, the use of a flatpick will enhance the "raunch" of this particular piece.

Open E Tuning   *By Robert Johnson. As played by Elmore James*

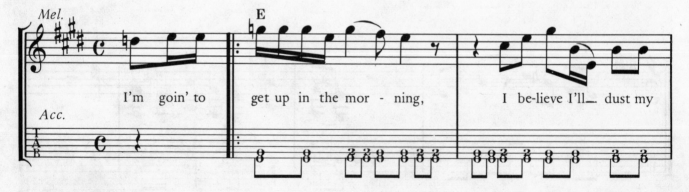

I'm gonna write a letter, telephone every town I know, (2X)
If I can't find her in West Helena, she must be in East Munroe, I know.

I don't want no woman wants every down-town man she meets, (2X)
She's a no-good domey, the shouldn't (al)'low her on the street.

I believe, I believe I'll go back home, (2X)
You can mistreat me here Babe, but you can't when I go home.

And I'm gettin' up in the morning, I believe I'll dust my broom,
I'm gettin' up in the morning, I believe I'll dust my broom,
Girl friend, the black man you been lovin', girl friend, can get my room.

I'm gonna call up China, see is my good gal over there, (2X)
If I can't find her in the Philippine Islands, she must be in Ethiopia somewhere.

Dust My Broom

Licks and Exercises in Open E Tuning

Undoubtedly, there are countless possibilities in lead slide guitar, beside the relatively simple *Dust My Broom* lick. The remaining material in this chapter will focus on some of these possibilities.

I suppose the major difference in playing lead slide as opposed to the more traditional style of bottleneck is the phrasing and approach that is used. Since electric slide is usually played louder than the other styles we've covered, greater control and restraint is required on the part of the musician. This is not to say that one must always feel inhibited with an electric guitar, but rather that you can reach higher *peaks* when so desired depending upon the amount of control exercised.

Of course, all of the traditional E tuning licks you're already familiar with can be transferred to electric guitar. The new licks and exercises that follow are based on the same scales that were used in the Traditional Bottleneck section, but some of the phrasing, note positions, and the various changes of mood should hopefully present some fresh challenges and ideas for you.

Lead Licks

113

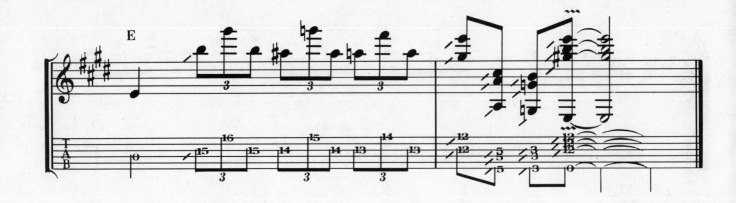

LOVE IN VAIN

Love in Vain is a perfect example of what a lead slide guitarist can do with a traditional blues song in open G tuning. Originally recorded in 1937 by Robert Johnson, The Rolling Stones recently cut a version of it on their *Let it Bleed* album. The song is transcribed as Johnson sang it, but the accompaniment and solo are written with a lead slide approach. The chords are from The Rolling Stones' version, and some of the licks are reminiscent of Keith Richards' slide work. The original key of Johnson's recording is A .

Love in Vain

By Robert Johnson.
Arranged and adapted by Arlen Roth

Open G Tuning

And I fol- lowed her to the sta - tion

with her suit - case in my hand,— And I

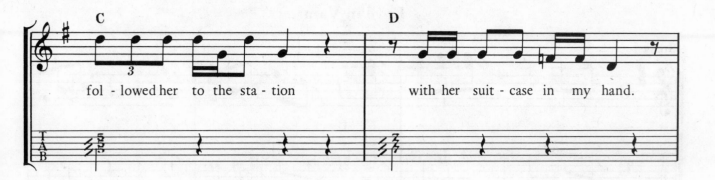

fol - lowed her to the sta - tion   with her suit - case in my hand.

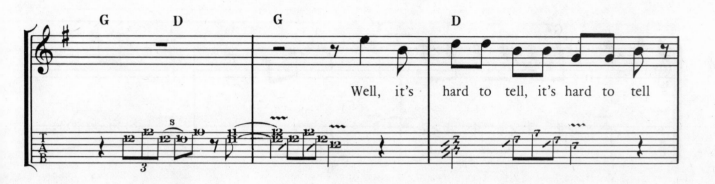

Well, it's   hard to tell, it's hard to tell

when all your love's in   vain,___   All   my love's in vain,___   when the

Fine

When the rain rolled up to the station I looked her in the eye, (2x)
Well I was lonesome, I felt so lonesome, and I could not help but cry.
All my love's in vain.

When the train it left the station, there was two lights on behind (2x)
Well the blue light was my blues, and the red light was my mind.
All my love's in vain.

Umm, Willie Mae,
Umm, Willie Mae,
Umm, umm—
All my love's in vain.

Love in Vain

Slide Guitar in Standard Tuning

Over the past few years, an increasing number of my students have been showing a growing interest in learning bottleneck in standard tuning. The reason for this recent rise in the popularity of standard tuning slide is probably because so many well-known lead guitarists are now working slide parts into their standard tuning solos. Therefore, its most convenient aspect is that you can simply pick up the slide and immediately add a new dimension to your playing, minus the limitations imposed upon your normal fretting by open tunings.

As far as overall slide sound is concerned, however, I should point out that certain technical disadvantages possibly may outweigh the convenience of playing in this tuning. One shortcoming lies in the fact that since you are playing without an open tuning, the notes of the scales we have been using are farther apart. This limitation tends to create a great degree of *searching* for notes than when utilizing an open tuning *box pattern* scale for improvising. Another disadvantage that can be particularly annoying is that since there is no major chord created by several strings played together at the same fret (with the exception of the open B, G and D strings which remain unchanged for open G tuning), overtones due to the sounding of undesired strings are usually dissonant, or off key. These often unavoidable overtones can be due to over active slide section, improper damping, or just right hand inaccuracy, and can be quite discouraging to someone who is a newcomer to standard tuning slide playing.

But after all is said and done, it is still apparent that this style of bottleneck is catching on, and has worked quite well for many of today's most influential lead guitarists. I'm sure that with a certain degree of work you can reach the kind of musical standards that these people have been achieving, and maybe even set some new goals in the process.

Standard Tuning Blues Scale

When playing lead guitar, there are several blues scales that I improvise with, but I have found only one of these scales to be well-suited to slide playing. The major reasons for its convenience is that while it covers a large area of the neck, it retains the smooth flow of a *box pattern* scale, and in fact has a smaller box pattern of its own. Here is the scale in the key of E with a diagram showing the position of its *box* notes:

Blues Pattern

Strings tuned to:

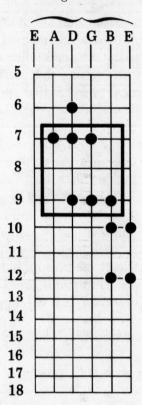

Licks and Exercises in Standard Tuning

Licks and Turnarounds

The majority of the licks we will be working with are based on the blues scale you have just seen. However, there are a few riffs here that venture away from this pattern, including some open position *hammer-on* licks. Remember, also, that in standard tuning, slide right hand damping and accuracy, as well as careful slide work, are critical in making these runs come off cleanly:

Blues Licks

Turnaround Licks

121

These next four exercises are the most difficult pieces to execute. They utilize all the fine points of slide playing that I have discussed so far, and certainly leave little to be desired as far as the gymnastics of standard tuning slide are concerned.

Again, I must stress the importance of right hand damping in deriving the most from these exercises. But above all, considering all of that slide playing already under your belt, you should now be able to just pick up your guitar, play these pieces, and enjoy yourself in the process.

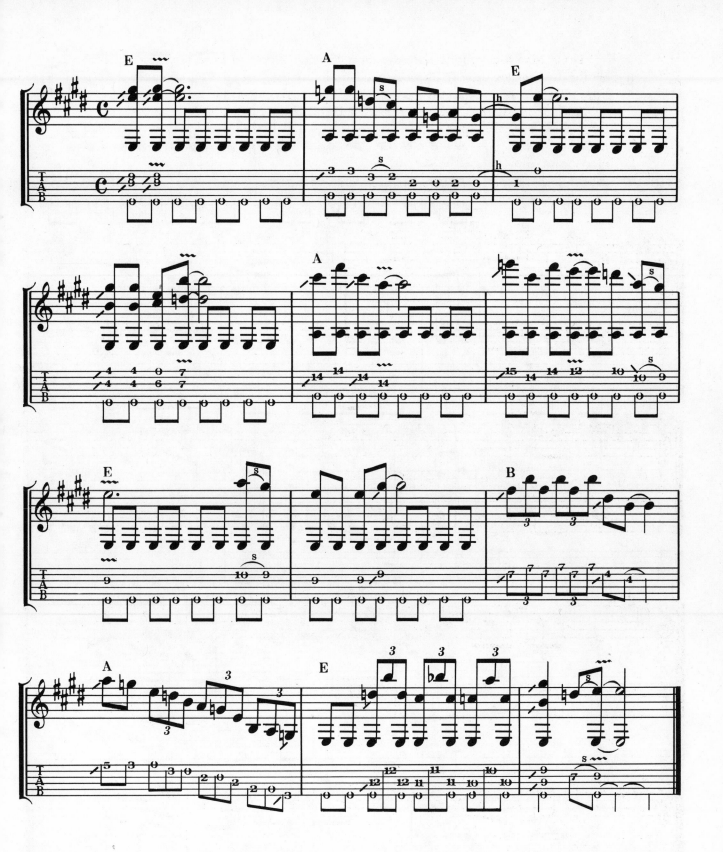

In Conclusion

In deciding on the choice of material in this book, my main intention was to present slide guitar as another means by which a guitarist's feeling may be expressed. No doubt, I've broken bottleneck down into its technical aspects, but I still feel that the bottleneck guitars' sound should remain ultimately one of emotion, rather than of technical wizardry. Now, where to go from here? I would first suggest that you seek out other musicians and slide guitarists to play with. This communication with other people through your music is truly the most fulfilling part of being a guitarist. Listening to recordings of the great bottleneck artists, past and present, will also bring to light more of the possibilities available to you.

But above all, I hope that the sharing of some of my musical ideas with you has aided in your developing a deeper understanding of what your guitar, and playing music, means to you. I'm happy to have had the opportunity to tell it to you my way, now it's time for you to say it your way. Good luck!

Johnny Winter

Discography

Although there are many albums containing slide guitar work, the following discography lists some of the most interesting and important bottleneck playing available on record. If you're interested in further developing your bottleneck style, I would certainly recommend making a study of these artists.

Traditional Bottleneck

Robert Johnson/*King of the Delta Blues Singers Vols. 1 and 2* (Columbia CL 1654, C30034)

Son House/*Father of Folk Blues* (Columbia CS 9217)

Charley Patton/*Founder of the Delta Blues* (Yazoo L 1020)

Tampa Rcd/*Bottleneck Guitar—1928-1937* (Yazoo L 1039) and *Guitar Wizards, 1926-1935* (Yazoo L 1016)

Country Blues Bottleneck Guitar Classics (Yazoo L 1026)

Blind Willie McTell/*1927-1933, The Early Years* (Yazoo L 1005)

Electric Rhythm and Blues Slide

Elmore, or "Elmo" James/*The Sky is Crying* (Sphere Sound LP 7002) and *Elmore James, John Brim—Whose Muddy Shoes* (Chess 1537)

J. B. Hutto and his Hawks/*Chicago—The Blues—Today, Vol. 1* (Vanguard VSD 79216)

Homesick James and his Dusters/*Chicago—The Blues—Today, Vol. 2* (Vanguard VSD 79217)

Contemporary Lead Slide

Ry Cooder/*Into the Purple Valley* (Reprise MS 2052) and *Boomer's Story* (Reprise MS 2117)

The Rolling Stones with Mick Taylor/*Let it Bleed* (London, NPS 4) and *Sticky Fingers* with Ry Cooder (Rolling Stones Records, COC 59100)

Duane Allman/*Eat a Peach* (Capricorn 2CP0102) and *An Anthology* (Capricorn 2CP 0108)

Note:

If you wish to further your study of slide guitar, I have recorded a taped bottleneck instruction series that is now available. For information write to: Homespun Tapes, Box 694, Woodstock, N.Y. 12498

Left to right — Dobro, pedal steel, lap steel, Hawaiian steel and National steel